*To Val*
*a fine player on the field of life*
*with our love from*
*Frank &*
*[...]*
*11/2/1994*

Other mini books in this series:

Cat Quotations          Teddy Bear Quotations
Golf Quotations         Music Lover's Quotations
Horse Quotations        Book Lover's Quotations
Love Quotations         Garden Lover's Quotations

Published simultaneously in 1992 by Exley Publications in
Great Britain and Exley Giftbooks in the USA.
Reprinted 1992
**Third printing 1993**
Copyright © Helen Exley 1992
**Series editor Helen Exley**

ISBN 1-85015-319-1

A copy of the CIP data is available from the British Library on
request.

**Pictures edited by Helen Exley.**
**Words selected by Elizabeth Cotton.**
Designed by Pinpoint Design Company.
Pictures researched by Image Select.
Words researched by Margaret Montgomery
**Printed and bound in Hungary**

Exley Publications Ltd, 16 Chalk Hill, Watford,
Herts WD1 4BN, United Kingdom.
Exley Giftbooks, 359 East Main Street, Suite 3D,
Mount Kisco, NY 10549, USA

Exley Publications is very grateful to the following individuals
and organizations for permission to reproduce their pictures:
Advertising Archive, AKG Archive, David Rayvern Allen,
Bridgeman Art Library, E. T. Archive, Mary Evans Picture
Library, Fine Art Society London, Marylebone Cricket Club,
Ann Ronan Picture Library, Southampton Art Gallery.

# CRICKET
## QUOTATIONS

A COLLECTION OF
FINE PAINTINGS AND THE
BEST CRICKET QUOTES

**EXLEY**
MT. KISCO, NEW YORK • WATFORD, UK

"Cricket to us was more than play,
It was a worship in the summer sun."

EDMUND BLUNDEN
*from "Pride of the Village"*

– ◆ –

"[Cricket] Heroes in fact die with one's youth.
They are pinned like butterflies to the setting
board of early memories – the time when skies
were always blue, the sun shone, and the air
was filled with the sounds and scents of grass
being cut."

ALAN ROSS
*from "Cricket Heroes"*

"The crack of bat against ball amid that
humming and buzzing of summer
sound is still to me a note of pure joy
that raised haunting memories of
friends and happy days."

LADY BALDWIN

## GENTLEMEN

"Go to Lord's and analyse the crowd. There are all sorts and conditions of men there round the ropes – bricklayers, bank clerks, soldiers, postmen, and stockbrokers. And in the pavilion are QCs, artists, archdeacons and leader-writers. Bad men, good men, workers and idlers, are all there, and all at one in their keenness over the game . . . cricket brings the most opposite characters and the most diverse lives together. Anything that puts very many different kinds of people on a common ground must promote sympathy and kindly feelings."

PRINCE RANJITSINHJI

"When 'it isn't cricket' has become an anachronism and a smear, cricket will be close to its deathbed."

J. M. KILBURN

"The very word 'cricket' has become a synonym for all that is true and honest. To say 'that is not cricket' implies something underhand, something not in keeping with the best ideals."

SIR PELHAM WARNER

– ◆ –

"Cricket? It civilises people and creates good gentlemen. I want everyone to play cricket in Zimbabwe. I want ours to be a nation of gentlemen."

ROBERT MUGABE
Prime Minister of Zimbabwe

– ◆ –

WILLS's Cigarettes.

MR. K.S. RANJITSINHJI,
SUSSEX.

"A game is exactly what is made of it by the character of the men playing it. New laws, new ways of preparing wickets, new schemes of reckoning championships – these external things do not matter."

SIR NEVILLE CARDUS

– ♦ –

"In the end it is only the camaraderie of the team, the lifelong friendships which you forge, and the opportunity for interesting sorties outside the grind of the cricket grounds which make the experience worthwhile."

BILL O'REILLY

– ♦ –

But what care I? It's the game that calls me –
Simply to be on the field of play;
How can it matter what fate befalls me,
With ten good fellows and one good day!

A. A. MILNE

"Village cricket spread fast through the land.
In those days, before it became scientific,
cricket was the best game in the world to
watch – each ball a potential crisis."

GEORGE M. TREVELYAN

"Few things are more deeply rooted in the
collective imagination of the English than the
village cricket match. It stirs a romantic
illusion about the rustic way of life,
it suggests a tranquil and unchanging order
in an age of bewildering flux, and it persuades
a lot of townsfolk that that is where they
would rather be."

GEOFFREY MOORHOUSE

"Village cricketers are too kindly to drop you
with abruptness at the end of your career."

ERIC N. SIMONS

## LORD'S – THE MECCA OF CRICKET

"For your good cricketer the ends of
the earth have come to a resting-point at
Lord's, and wherever he may be at the

fall of a summer's day his face should
turn religiously towards Lord's."

SIR NEVILLE CARDUS

## MORE THAN A GAME

"Cricket – it's more than a game.
It's an institution."

THOMAS HUGHES
*from "Tom Brown's Schooldays"*

"But after all it's not the winning that matters,
is it? Or is it? It's – to coin a word – the
amenities that count: the smell of the
dandelions, the puff of the pipe, the click of
the bat, the rain on the neck, the chill down
the spine, the slow, exquisite coming on of
sunset and dinner and rheumatism."

ALASTAIR COOKE

"Long ago I discovered there was more to life
than cricket: and more to cricket than runs
and wickets."

DAVID FOOT
*from "Cricket's Unholy Trinity"*

"Life is an elaborate metaphor for cricket."

MARVIN COHEN

> "The British 'Sphere of Influence' – the cricket ball."
>
> from Mr. Punch's Book of Sport

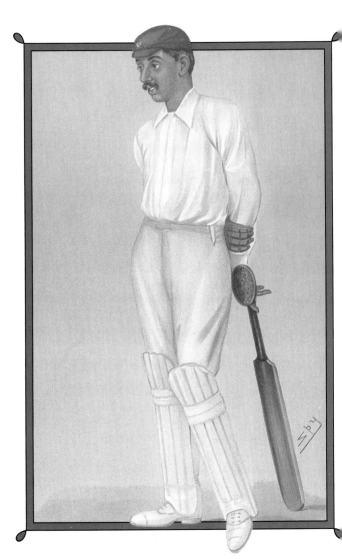

"One fascination of cricket is that it never ceases to fascinate. To become a devotee in childhood means being hooked for life. Happily it is an addiction for which there is no need of legislation nor government health warnings."

DAVID RAYVERN ALLEN
*from "Cricket. An Illustrated History"*

— ♦ —

"For a long time we dreamed of a real leather ball, and at last my brother had one for his birthday. The feel of the leather, the stitching round it, the faint gold letters stamped upon it, the touch of the seam, the smell of it, all affected me so deeply that I still have that ache of beauty when I hold a cricket ball."

ALISON UTTLEY
*from "Carts and Candlesticks"*

— ♦ —

No. 6082    PUNCH, MAY 29 1957    Vol. CCXXXII

# Punch

9d

smilby

## FROM THE WEST INDIES

"The full implications of the religious teaching
may have passed me by, but there was one
overriding compensation which made those
three hours absolutely compulsory. We played
cricket. Needless to say, I never missed
Sunday School, bible in one hand and cricket
ball in the other."

MALCOLM MARSHALL
*from "Marshall Arts"*

— ◆ —

"The first vision that comes to mind as we think
of West Indies cricket is of joyful noise, a bat
flailing the air, the ball whizzing here, there,
everywhere, stumps flying, shining black faces
and mouths laughing white-toothed."

SIR NEVILLE CARDUS

— ◆ —

"Cricket can be a bridge and a glue. . . .
Cricket for peace is my mission."

PRESIDENT ZIA
of Pakistan

"It is true to say there is scarcely a part of the
globe that has not witnessed cricket in one
form or another: every continent – including
Antarctica, up mountain, down valley, on sea
and on land, on beach and on pavement,
outdoors and indoors."

DAVID RAYVERN ALLEN
from "Cricket. An Illustrated History"

"On the plains of India, in Australia
(as some of our English cricketers have
learnt to their cost), in Egypt, wherever
Englishmen go, there cricket finds a home
and a hearty welcome."

P. H. DITCHFIELD

### THE CAPTAIN'S ROLE

"As harrowing occupations go,
there can't be much to choose between
the Australian cricket captaincy and social
work on skid row."

DOUG IBBOTSON

– ◆ –

*A captain's role* – "A PR officer, agricultural
consultant, psychiatrist, accountant,
nursemaid and diplomat."

DOUG INSOLE

– ◆ –

"When you win the toss – bat.
If you are in doubt, think about it – then bat.
If you have very big doubts, consult a
colleague – then bat."

W. G. GRACE

"Cricket is a game of the most terrifying
stresses with more luck about it than any
other game I know. They call it a team game,
but in fact it is the loneliest game of all."

JOHN ARLOTT
*from "Another Word from Arlott"*

"It is a cussed game. It can show you glimpses
of beauty in a stroke perfectly played,
perhaps, and then it throws you back into the
trough of mediocrity. Only the most
phlegmatic or those who don't give a damn or
those with unshakeable belief survive these
upheavals easily."

PETER ROEBUCK
*from "It Never Rains"*

"Cricket is quite a gentle, harmless game, but
he is a lucky man who has not to sweat some
blood before he's done with it."

J. C. SNAITH

## A GAME OF CONTRASTS

"This game preys on doubt. It is a precarious game. Form, luck, confidence are transitory things. It's never easy to work out why they have so inexplicably deserted you."

PETER ROEBUCK
*from "It Never Rains"*

— ♦ —

"The game itself is a capricious blend of elements, static and dynamic, sensational and somnolent. You can never take your eyes away from a cricket match for fear of missing a crisis. For hours it will proceed to a rhythm as lazy as the rhythm of an airless day. . . . A sudden bad stroke, a good ball, a marvellous catch, and the crowd is awake; a bolt has been hurled into our midst from a clear sky."

SIR NEVILLE CARDUS
*from "Cardus on Cricket"*

— ♦ —

OUR CRICKETING GUESTS

"His bat was part of his nervous system."

HAROLD PINTER
on Sir Len Hutton

— ♦ —

*On facing the "quicks"* – "To have some idea
what it's like, stand in the outside lane of a
motorway, get your mate to drive his car at
you at 95 mph and wait until he's 12 yards
away, before you decide which way to jump."

GEOFF BOYCOTT

— ♦ —

"Like all cricket devotees I have many,
many times shared with all around me
that infectious, 'breathless hush' tension
as a batsman, however well-set, however
self-possessed, has to face up to the
obligation of scoring that hundredth run."

BEN TRAVERS

— ♦ —

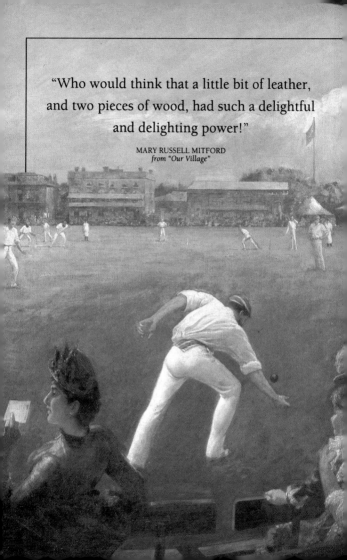

"Who would think that a little bit of leather, and two pieces of wood, had such a delightful and delighting power!"

MARY RUSSELL MITFORD
*from "Our Village"*

Ready!

LANCE THACKE

"The greatest duffer at the game is the most
enthusiastic."

R. A. FITZGERALD

— ◆ —

". . . The curious thing is that it attracts the
incompetents as well, those who never make a
run and cannot bowl, and yet, doomed only to
dreary waiting in the pavilion and to fatiguing
fielding, they turn up punctually on every
occasion, hoping for the best, and even, such
is the human heart's buoyancy, expecting it."

JOHN ARLOTT

— ◆ —

"What is this lure . . . that cricket exercises . . .
the passion for [it] is in our blood. Small boys
have it, youths have it, grown men have it,
old men have it; and no amount of
disappointment, no ducks, can change it.

E. V. LUCAS

"We have nothing against man cricketers.
Some of them are quite nice people, even
though they don't win as often as we do."

RACHAEL HEYHOE-FLINT

"Some women's cricket at club level is played
solely for enjoyment and is perhaps better not
seen by the public – but then so is some men's
cricket for that matter."

RACHAEL HEYHOE-FLINT and NETTA RHEINBERG
*from "Fair Play"*

"Women will always play for the love of the
game and there will be no professional female
cricketers. At the same time, the enjoyment of
the game must go hand in hand with skill,
ability and flair."

RACHAEL HEYHOE-FLINT and NETTA RHEINBERG
*from "Fair Play"*

"Cricket remains for me the game of games, the sanspareil, the great metaphor, the best marriage ever devised of mind and body. None of the other sports . . . neither soccer nor rugby, nor golf, nor tennis – can begin to touch it. For me it remains the Proust of pastimes, the subtlest and most poetic, the most past-and-present; whose beauty can lie equally in days, in a whole, or in one tiny phrase, a blinding split second."

JOHN FOWLES
*from "Vain Memories" in "Quick Singles"*

— ♦ —

"What is human life but a game of cricket?"

THE DUKE OF DORSET

1979 International Year of the Child 50c

Commonwealth of Dominica

OUTSTANDING ACHIEVEMENTS IN CRICKET

VIVI RICHARDS

ANDY ROBERTS

1976 SPECIAL EVENTS

ANTIGUA 50c

## AN ADDICTION

"There is a widely held and quite erroneous
belief that cricket is just another game."

H. R. H. THE DUKE OF EDINBURGH

— ◆ —

"I tend to believe that cricket is the greatest
thing that God ever created on Earth . . .
certainly greater than sex although sex isn't
too bad either. But everyone knows
which comes first when it's a question
of cricket or sex."

HAROLD PINTER

"It's a funny kind of month, October. For the
really keen cricket fan it's when you realise
that your wife left you in May."

DENIS NORDEN

"To all who love cricket, and to the
Coarse Cricketer in particular, the
winter is always long."

SPIKE HUGHES

"It is surely the loveliest scene in England and the most disarming sound. From the ranks of the unseen dead for ever passing along our country lanes, the Englishman falls out for a moment to look over the gate of the cricket field and smile."

SIR JAMES BARRIE

"The fellows were practising long shies and bowling lobs and slow twisters. In the soft grey silence he could hear the bump of the balls: and from here and from there through the quiet air the sound of the cricket bats: pick, pack, pock, puck: like drops of water in a fountain falling softly in the brimming bowl."

JAMES JOYCE
from "A Portrait of the Artist as a Young Man"

## HINTS

*To the Team by their Captain*

1. Don't practise on opponent's ground
   before match begins.

   This can only give them confidence.

2. Each man, when he goes in, to tap the
   ground with his bat.

3. Should you hit the ball, run at once.
   Don't stop to cheer.

4. No batsman is allowed to choose his own
   bowler. You needn't think it.

5. Partridge, when bowling, keep your eye on
   square-leg.

6. Square-leg, when Partridge is bowling.
   Keep your eye on him.

7. If bowled first ball, pretend that you only
   came out for the fun of the thing, and then go
   away and sit by yourself behind the hedge.

J. M. BARRIE

No. 6292     PUNCH APRIL 19 1961     Vol. CCXL

# Punch

9d

HARGREAVES

" 'Cricket was intended to be played between 22 sportsmen for their own pleasure; it was never meant to be the vehicle for international competition, huge crowds and headline news – otherwise it wouldn't have been given a code of laws with such gaps as you could drive through with a coach and horses.' "

B. H. LYON

— ◆ —

"There ought to be some other means of reckoning quality in this the best and loveliest of games; the scoreboard is an ass."

SIR NEVILLE CARDUS

— ◆ —

"There's more ways of getting out than is shown in t'rules."

WILFRED RHODES

— ◆ —

"It is that cricket field that, in all the sharp and bitter moments of life as they come to me now, gives me a sense of wholesome proportion: 'At least I am not playing cricket!'"

JOHN COWPER POWYS

– ♦ –

*On seeing a game of football* – "I do love cricket – it's so very English."

SARAH BERNHARDT

– ♦ –

"Personally, I have always looked upon cricket as organised loafing."

WILLIAM TEMPLE

– ♦ –

"For all who were playing and watching there was nothing in mind beyond the next ball, the challenge of the moment, the absorption in good-natured contest. Time stood still in a distillation of delight."

J. M. KILBURN
*from "Thanks to Cricket"*

"As I think of those cricketing days I believe
that the greatest joy in life was playing in the
home meadow by the river on that soft turf,
with the echoing hills guarding the circle of
green. Batting was a hazardous job, but bowling
and fielding I loved. . . . I felt on top of the
world as I waited, loose-limbed, free, on tip-toe,
ready to dart forward, concentrated upon the
game, yet aware of those hills and the shining,
tossing river, of the scent of hay from the
meadows around us, and the blue sky above."

ALISON UTTLEY

"Cricket in high summer played with the
mind of the true lover of it conscious the
whole while that all this happy life is about
him – that cricket is just a corner in the
teeming garden of the year."

SIR NEVILLE CARDUS

CRICKET. You can't bowl me out.

. . . The school clock crawled, but cricket
thoughts would fill
The last slow lesson-hour deliciously
(Drone on, O teacher: you can't trouble me)
'Kent will be out by now'... (Well if you choose
To keep us here while cricket's in the air,
You must expect our minds to wander loose.)

THOMAS MOULT

"My first game of cricket was played in the
street when I was four years of age. The
pavement was our pitch, the front wall of a
house the back-stop and a biscuit-tin
the wicket."

M. A. NOBLE

"Should every county cricket ground be
closed and never another shilling of gate-
money leave our pockets, cricket would still
be in England's lifeblood drawing its
undismayable devotees from every section of
the nation: the cricket that has such a hold on
the young that they take their bats to bed with
them, and on the old that they cannot see half
a dozen urchins in the street, with only a
lamp-post for stumps without pausing for a
minute or two to watch: . . ."

E. V. LUCAS
*from "English Leaves"*

"In the very breadth of its humanity, its sweet simplicities, its open-air fragrance and charm, the game of cricket appeals to nearly all men."

A. E. KNIGHT
*from "The Complete Cricketer"*

— ◆ —

"When somebody told me that a man once died from excitement at a cricket match and another spectator gnawed the handle off his umbrella in a nervous spasm, it was hardly a shock. It seemed a pleasing way to die."

JACK POLLARD
*from "The Boundary Book of Cricket Second Innings"*

— ♦ —

"Medieval theologians used to dispute how the angels in heaven spent their time, when not balancing on needle points and singing anthems to the Lord. I know. They slump glued to their clouds, glasses at the ready, as the Archangel Michael (that well-known slasher) and stonewalling St Peter open against the Devil's XI. It could not be Heaven, otherwise."

JOHN FOWLES
*from "Vain Memories" in "Quick Singles"*

— ♦ —

When all the nations throng
the Judgement hill
Where Peter, with his great keys,
guards the wicket,
England, in lazy flannels lounging, will
Question the Fisherman:
Did you play cricket?

IRISH VERSE

"Oh God, if there be
cricket in heaven, let
there also be rain."

SIR ALEC DOUGLAS HOME